Diego RIVERA

AN ARTIST FOR THE PEOPLE

SUSAN GOLDMAN RUBIN

ABRAMS BOOKS FOR YOUNG READERS • NEW YORK

Diego Rivera used the word *Indian* when speaking of the *campesinos*, the indigenous peoples of Mexico, who typically would never be the subject of fine art. He used *Indian* respectfully and affectionately, referring to the descendants of the ancient pre-Columbian cultures. Therefore, I have kept the word *Indian* in the text, to be true to Rivera's point of view. —S.G.R.

Library of Congress Cataloging-in-Publication Data

Rubin, Susan Goldman.
Diego Rivera : an artist for the people / by Susan Goldman Rubin.
pages cm
Includes bibliographical references and index.
ISBN 978-0-8109-8411-0
1. Rivera, Diego, 1886–1957—Juvenile literature. 2. Painters—Mexico—Biography—Juvenile literature.
I. Title.
ND259.R5R83 2013
759.972—dc23
[B]
2012010022

Printed and bound in China
10 9 8 7 6 5 4 3 2 1

Abrams Books for Young Readers are available at special discounts when purchased in quantity for premiums and promotions as well as fundraising or educational use. Special editions can also be created to specification. For details, contact specialsales@abramsbooks.com or the address below.

THE ART OF BOOKS SINCE 1949
115 West 18th Street
New York, NY 10011
www.abramsbooks.com

To PEGGY and SEAN McELGUNN

Self-Portrait, 1941.
Rivera holds a
note, written in
Spanish, dedicating
his self-portrait to
Irene Rich, who had
requested a painting
from him.

When Diego Rivera arrived in Europe to study art, his appearance caught everyone's attention. "I was twenty years old, over six feet tall, and weighed three hundred pounds," he said. Children in the streets of Paris would shout when they saw him lumbering along with his big Mexican walking stick, wide-brimmed hat, and bulging eyes. Rivera said, "People I love most think I look like a frog."

Rivera thought so too. Over the years he did many self-portraits that emphasized his froggy eyes and full lips. He dedicated one of these self-portraits to Irene Rich, a movie actress he knew in California. Rivera wrote the inscription on a piece of paper that he holds in the painting, a device he borrowed from Mexican colonial art.

As a young man in Paris, Rivera often posed for his artist friends. Smiling, he boasted that he had eaten the flesh of cadavers while taking an anatomy class in Mexico City. And his friends almost believed him. Affectionately, they dubbed him "the genial cannibal" because of his tall tales.

Like other art students in the early twentieth century, Rivera copied works in the Louvre Museum, painted outdoors, and attended lectures and exhibitions. Yet, after four years of studying and imitating European painters and styles, Rivera felt "restless, dissatisfied, impatient." His work looked "academic and empty."

"What I knew best and felt most deeply was my own country, Mexico," he said. Rivera wanted to create a new kind of art for and about his people. "The new art . . . would not be [displayed in] a museum or gallery" but in everyday places: "post offices, schools, theaters, railroad stations, public buildings."

"And so," wrote Rivera, "I arrived at mural painting." He also wrote, "The secret of my best work is that it is Mexican."

ABOVE: Diego Rivera at the age of four with his toy train, in Guanajuato, Mexico, ca. 1890.

OPPOSITE: *The Boy with the Taco*, 1932. In this lithograph, a form of printmaking, Rivera portrayed a peasant child and his hungry dog.

Rivera was born in Guanajuato, Mexico, on December 8, 1886. He had a twin brother, Carlos, who died at the age of eighteen months. When Rivera was two years old, he became thin and sickly, and his parents worried that he would die like his brother. So they sent him to the country with his Indian nurse to stay in her village and benefit from the fresh mountain air.

When Rivera returned to his parents' home two years later, he continued to draw as he had before. "As far back as I can remember," he said, "I was drawing. Almost as soon as my fat baby fingers could grasp a pencil, I was marking up walls, doors, and furniture." His father, a teacher, gave him a special room in the house covered with black canvas as high as he could reach. This was his "studio."

"Here I made my earliest 'murals,'" said Rivera.

One of his first drawings showed a locomotive chugging uphill. Rivera loved mechanical toys, especially trains, and wanted to be an engineer when he grew up. Everyone in Guanajuato called him "the engineer" because he spent hours at the railroad station. He made friends with some of the railroad workers. "They would take me for short rides in the cab," he said, "even allowing me to hold the throttle and blow the whistle."

When Rivera was five years old, his sister María was born. On that day, his aunt told him a train would deliver the baby in a package. Rivera went to the station, eagerly awaiting the baby's arrival. At last, the stationmaster told him that his little sister had arrived. "We sent her home some time ago in a beautiful little box," he said.

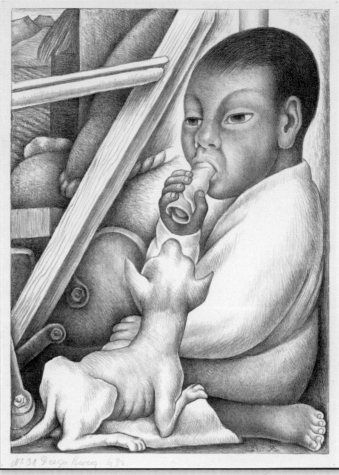

Rivera ran home and saw the baby. He searched through the house for the box she had supposedly come in but found nothing. The adults had lied! Furious, he marched off to bed without eating dinner. The next day, his father told him how babies are born and gave him books on the subject. "I began to teach myself to read," said Rivera.

A year later, Rivera's mother took him and his sister to Mexico City. Soon Rivera's father joined them and looked for a job. "The home we found was a poor one in a poor neighborhood," wrote Rivera. There was no longer room for him to have a studio, and for a while he almost stopped drawing. Rivera came down with scarlet fever, then typhoid. During his illnesses, his Aunt Totota told him stories and read to him. As Rivera got better, he asked her to teach him how to write.

For two years, he attended schools run by the Catholic Church. At age ten, he was eligible to enter the National Preparatory School. But Rivera knew that he wanted to be an artist. Already he showed remarkable skill as a draftsman. A pencil sketch of his mother was so accurate—and so unflattering—that she destroyed it. Rivera demanded to go to art school. Finally, his parents agreed to let him attend preparatory school in the daytime and the San Carlos Academy of Fine Arts at night.

For the next two years, Rivera worked hard. He completed elementary school and won a scholarship at San Carlos. Not yet thirteen, he began studying art full-time.

In those days, Mexicans regarded Europe as the art center of the world. San Carlos students followed the classical tradition of copying plaster casts and printed reproductions of the casts. Rivera hated it. "The further I progressed in the academic European forms, the less I liked them and the more I was drawn to the old Mexican art," he said.

Around this time, he met the folk artist José Guadalupe Posada, a printmaker. Posada made lithographs and etchings that illustrated Mexican songs and stories and commented on politics and everyday life. Posada produced these pictures for the common people, who were mostly poor and illiterate. They could not read words, but they could "read" pictures. The etchings, which Posada printed on colored tissue paper, were sold cheaply by traveling musicians.

Every afternoon, Rivera visited Posada's shop, located near the art school. Fascinated, he pored over Posada's prints of the lively skeletons called *calaveras*. Posada depicted hundreds of *calaveras* for the Mexican holiday the Day of the Dead, or El Dia dc los Muertos. One print shows skeletons playing music and dancing in a cantina. Another features a skeleton wearing a plumed hat and is titled *La Calavera Catrina*, which means "the well-dressed [or elegant] skull." These images stayed with Rivera. Years later, in an autobiographical mural, he honored Posada by painting a portrait of him walking arm in arm with *La Catrina*. Looking back, Rivera regarded Posada

La Calavera Catrina (left) and *El jarabe en ultratumba* (*The Folk Dance Beyond the Grave*, below), by José Guadalupe Posada. Posada created a series of *calaveras*, frisky, humorous skeletons dressed as contemporary figures. They were especially popular for Day of the Dead celebrations.

as one of his best teachers. "It was he who revealed to me the inherent beauty in the Mexican people," Rivera wrote.

When Rivera was sixteen, he left the academy to roam the countryside and paint landscapes. But he was dissatisfied with the results. Finally, he returned to San Carlos to complete his last two years of formal training. He graduated with honors. Yet he knew he needed to learn more. He began to dream of going to Europe. But how could he afford it?

According to family legend, Rivera's father, now an inspector in the National Department of Public Health, asked Joaquín Obregón González, the governor of the state of Guanajuato, to give his son a scholarship. The governor refused. So Rivera's father took Rivera on a trip to another state called Vera Cruz, and they met with its governor, Teodoro A. Dehesa. "We Veracruzanos know how to appreciate art," said Governor Dehesa, and he agreed to pay Rivera's expenses for studying abroad. So in January 1907, Rivera sailed to Spain.

In Madrid, he studied with Eduardo Chicharro, a leading portrait painter. Chicharro and other Spaniards nicknamed Rivera "the Mexican" because of the large sombrero he wore. Rivera said his head was so big that no "ordinary-size Spanish hat" would fit him. When he wasn't painting, he wandered through the Prado Museum and studied masterpieces by El Greco, Goya, and Velázquez. From time to time he sent his paintings to Governor Dehesa to show his progress. The governor was delighted.

But not Rivera. Sometimes after finishing a picture, he felt so unhappy with it that he beat his head against the wall and fled to the cafés to talk with his friends. Rivera's fellow painters told him about the exciting art scene in Paris, and in the spring of 1909 he traveled to France.

Las meninas (*The Maids of Honor*), 1656, by Diego Velázquez. Rivera studied this huge painting, ten feet high, in the Prado Museum in Madrid. It shows the young Infanta (Princess) Margarita surrounded by her maids of honor, two dwarfs, a dog, and Velázquez himself, on the left, holding his palette and paintbrush, as he paints their picture. The king and queen, reflected in the mirror, look on.

That summer, when he was twenty-two, Rivera visited the nearby country of Belgium. In the city of Brussels, he met a Russian artist named Angelina Beloff. They fell in love and became engaged. Back in Paris, Rivera continued painting. Although his work was admired and exhibited, he knew he was merely imitating European artists. "Suddenly," he wrote, "I felt an overmastering need to see my land and my people."

In September 1910, leaving Angelina behind, he sailed to Mexico. He had been away for almost four years, and his family and his sponsor, Governor Dehesa, greeted him warmly. In honor of Mexico's centenary, celebrating one hundred years of independence from Spain, Rivera prepared to exhibit his paintings at his old art school.

At that time, Mexico was ruled by President Porfirio Díaz, a dictator who helped industrialize and modernize the country but did little to help the lower classes. Under Díaz, electricity, telephones, and railroads came to Mexico, but Indian peasants and factory workers were treated unfairly. When another candidate ran against Díaz in the election of 1910, Díaz lost. But he proclaimed that he had won. This lie sparked anger among the people, and the Mexican Revolution began. It lasted for seven years. Rivera's old friend and mentor, Posada, created caricatures attacking the Díaz dictatorship and revealing the truth about the election fraud.

Rivera later claimed that he became involved in the revolt against Díaz. But in fact he devoted himself to painting. Toward the end of April 1911 he returned to Paris and his fiancée, Angelina.

Rivera, still working in a traditional, realistic manner, became interested in the "revolutionary" artistic style known as Cubism. The leader of the movement was Pablo Picasso, a Spanish-born painter living in Paris. Under Picasso's influence, Rivera switched to Cubism in 1913, and over the next few years he created hundreds of paintings in that style.

During the summer of 1914, while Rivera was busily painting, war broke out between the Allies (Great Britain, France, Italy, and Russia) and the Central Powers (Austria-Hungary, Germany, and Turkey). Rivera tried to join the French army, but he was turned down, maybe because of his huge size or his flat feet. As the Great War raged on, many foreign artists fled Paris, but Rivera and Angelina stayed. In August 1916, Angelina gave birth to their son. They named him Diego Junior.

Wartime shortages meant little food or fuel. Rivera and Angelina often went hungry in their unheated studio. The conditions were too hard for the baby. "There was no money for doctors or medicine," said Rivera.

Diego Junior became ill during a flu epidemic in October 1917 and died at the age of fourteen months. "This innocent death terribly depressed me," Rivera said. At the cemetery, he steadied Angelina, who was draped in heavy veils. Together they left flowers at the little grave.

Afterward, they moved to a different apartment, and he resumed painting.

In November 1918, the Great War (later known as World War I) ended. "Life was changing," said Rivera. "After the war nothing would be the same." He had given up Cubism and now searched for a more meaningful style of painting. A new friend, Dr. Élie Faure, who was a medical doctor as well as a poet and an art historian, encouraged Rivera to consider frescoes. They spent hours discussing the Italian medieval tradition of painting public art on walls. Rivera became enthusiastic and prepared for his "new career as a mural painter." The murals would be for the people of his country and not just a few rich collectors.

In January 1920, at the age of thirty-four, he packed up his paints and brushes and took off. "I went to Italy to study the frescoes of the old masters," he said. Angelina stayed behind in Paris, hoping that Rivera would soon return to her.

For the next year and a half, Rivera wandered through the cities of Florence, Padua, and Rome. Excitedly, he viewed the frescoes of the Renaissance artists Giotto, Uccello, and Michelangelo. He made more than three hundred sketches and even drew a picture of a muralist's scaffold in Florence to better understand its construction.

By 1921, Rivera was ready to return to Mexico alone to apply what he had learned. "The call of my country was stronger than ever," he wrote. Like his mentor Posada, Rivera wanted to teach the people of Mexico through pictures. At that time, most of the people still could not read or write. Murals would depict their history and also their visions of the future. Rivera would paint murals in public places where peasants and workers could view them.

Coming home thrilled Rivera. "All the colors I saw appeared to be heightened," he wrote. "In everything I saw a potential masterpiece—the crowds, the markets, the festivals . . . in every glowing face, in every luminous child . . .

"The very first sketch I completed amazed me. It was actually good! From then on, I worked confidently and contentedly."

Rivera found much changed upon his return to Mexico. President Díaz was no longer in office, the revolution was over, and Álvaro Obregón was now president. Obregón's new minister of education, José Vasconcelos, wanted to rebuild the country's culture. He organized a program of Mexican mural painting that included Rivera as well as David Siqueiros and José Clemente Orozco. "At last," wrote Rivera, "I was given a wall to cover at the National Preparatory School of the University of Mexico." This was the school where he had once been a student.

One day, while he was working in his studio, a friend introduced him to a girl from Guadalajara. Her name was Lupe Marín. Rivera was dazzled by Lupe's beauty and wild spirit. He had always liked the ladies, and the ladies had always liked him, despite his bulk and his habit of rarely taking a bath. Lupe offered to pose for him and modeled for the figure of Eve in his mural titled *Creation*. Though Rivera still corresponded

Il sogno di Gioacchino (*Joachim's Dream*), 1305, by Giotto. In the Scrovegni Chapel in Padua, Italy, Rivera viewed this early Renaissance fresco. The scene from the Christian story depicts Joachim (the husband of Anne and future father of Mary, the mother of Jesus) dreaming that an angel tells him he is going to be a father.

with Angelina, he never returned to her or asked her to come to Mexico. They never married. Instead, he married Lupe in June 1922 in a church ceremony.

That autumn, Rivera joined the Mexican Communist Party. It had been organized in 1911 to support the rights of miners, factory workers, and farmworkers. Within the party, Rivera formed the Union of Technical Workers, Painters, and Sculptors. Under the group's influence, "free art schools opened everywhere," said Rivera, "and thousands of workers and children of workers brought forth remarkable productions." He saw himself simply as a man in worn-out overalls, sitting on his scaffold, doing a job with a team of workers. By now, word of the Mexican mural movement had spread throughout the world, and painters came from other countries to participate.

When Rivera finished *Creation* in 1923, it aroused controversy. His fellow muralists Orozco and Siqueiros thought it symbolized Christian themes rather than portraying Mexican life. So to prepare for his next mural project, Rivera traveled through the country gathering material. On a trip to Tehuantepec in the state of Oaxaca, he was enthralled by the lush scenery and the Indians' everyday activities: weaving, grinding maize, and dancing *La Zandunga*. "Here, the people turned from their exhausting labors to their creative life, their joyful weddings, and their lively fiestas," he said.

Rivera used these themes in a mural for the new building of the Ministry of Education in Mexico City. For the first time, Indians and *campesinos* (people from the countryside) saw themselves as contributing to the culture of their country. Visitors to Mexico City came to see Rivera perching on a sagging beam and painting. He was becoming famous.

"As my work went on," he said, "I kept experimenting with and making discoveries in the techniques of painting on wall surfaces." Creating frescoes or murals meant painting on freshly laid plaster that was still wet.

Rivera's assistants prepared the surface with coats of plaster, the last consisting of

Dance in Tehuantepec, 1935. Rivera captured the lively rhythm of *La Zandunga*, a traditional folk dance from Oaxaca, Mexico.

a mixture of lime and marble dust. Then Rivera drew charcoal outlines to scale (that is, to exact size) directly on the plaster from his much smaller sketches, and painted the figures in gray. He did the final work in full color. His helpers ground the pigments and mixed them with distilled water to form a paste. Rivera put the colors on his palette (an old plate) and painted with a brush dipped in clean water. He had to work fast before the plaster dried. Each day when the light faded, he climbed down and studied what he had done. "If, as sometimes happens, I am dissatisfied," he said, "I have the whole area cleaned and a new coat of lime laid on. Then I redo the work the next day."

The Ministry of Education mural took Rivera four years to complete. Meanwhile, he worked on creating thirty-nine frescoes for the National Agricultural School in Chapingo, located just outside Mexico City. For this project, he began exploring themes of the history of Mexico before the Spanish Conquest.

Rivera became fascinated with Aztec culture and began collecting pre-Columbian sculptures. The small stone and terra-cotta figures inspired him to change his style. In his paintings, he now shaped the peasants in simplified forms like the sculptures. Often he sold the studies, or preliminary pieces, for his murals so he could afford more sculptures for his collection. His wife, Lupe, enraged that he was spending so much money on sculptures instead of groceries, once smashed a stone figure, ground it up, and fed it to Rivera in his soup!

Rivera traveled back and forth from Mexico City to Chapingo, from one job to the other, working seven days a week, to the point of exhaustion. While painting the school's chapel in Chapingo one day, he fell off his scaffold and fractured his skull. Over the next few months, Lupe nursed him back to health. During these busy years, Lupe gave birth to their daughters Guadalupe, known as "Picos," and Ruth, nicknamed "Chapo."

However, Rivera's marriage to Lupe began to fall apart. "I, unfortunately, was not a faithful husband," admitted Rivera. "I was always encountering women too desirable to resist."

One of those women was Tina Modotti, an Italian-born photographer from California. She posed for Rivera and took photos of his frescoes. They became romantically involved. Lupe was furious and divorced Rivera. By then his affair with Tina had ended. Lupe raised their daughters by herself.

In August 1927, Rivera traveled to the Soviet Union with a group of Communist

workers and artists to celebrate the tenth anniversary of the Soviet Revolution. On this trip he met Alfred Barr, an American who was about to become the first director of the Museum of Modern Art in New York City. Rivera showed Barr the photos of his frescoes, and Barr was impressed.

Rivera returned to Mexico in May 1928 and began planning a mural for the National Palace in Mexico City. The theme was the epic history of the Mexican people. Meanwhile, he completed the mural in the Ministry of Education.

While he was painting on the scaffold one day in the palace, a young woman came along and shouted up to him, "Diego, please come down from there!" He glanced at her and saw a slender woman with long hair and "thick eyebrows [that] met above her nose . . . like the wings of a blackbird."

Epic of the Mexican People: History of Mexico from the Conquest to 1930 (detail), 1929–31. This panel along a staircase in the National Palace, Mexico City, depicts Spanish conquistadors attacking the Aztecs. Rivera painted eleven more panels on the middle floor of the National Palace.

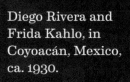

Diego Rivera and
Frida Kahlo, in
Coyoacán, Mexico,
ca. 1930.

When Rivera climbed down, she asked him to look at her paintings. "I want an absolutely straightforward opinion," she said.

"The canvases revealed an unusual energy of expression," he later said. "It was obvious to me that this girl was an authentic artist." He told her to continue painting.

She invited him to come to her house in Coyoacán the next Sunday to see more of her work. Rivera went, and a friendship blossomed between them. The woman's name was Frida Kahlo. She had just joined the Young Communist League, and he asked her to pose for a fresco panel in the Ministry of Education called *The Distribution of Arms*. He teased her as he painted a portrait of her handing out rifles and bayonets to fighting workers. "You have a dog-face," he said.

"And you have the face of a frog!" she said. From then on she affectionately called him *Carasapo* (Frog-face) or *Panza* (Fatbelly) and sometimes Fatso. Soon he was courting her. On August 21, 1929, they were married. Frida was twenty-two and Rivera was forty-two. He was more than six feet tall; she was five feet three inches. He weighed three hundred pounds; she weighed ninety-eight.

A month before the wedding, Rivera had started work on his mural in the National Palace. This monumental series of frescoes, located on the building's staircase, depicts the history of the Mexican people beginning with scenes of early Indian civilizations. A panel titled *History of Mexico from the Conquest to 1930* shows the Spanish conquistadors in helmets firing at the defeated Aztecs. The Aztecs appear to be toppling down the palace stairs. Rivera ingeniously used an artistic technique called trompe l'oeil, or "a trick to fool the eye," to make it seem as though the action was happening right there on the staircase. The entire project took him twenty years to complete! "I might leave it to paint other murals," he said, "but I kept returning to it . . . to make additions and changes."

While he was working on the National Palace frescoes, Rivera was expelled from the Mexican Communist Party. Members complained that he skipped meetings because he was too busy painting, and that when he did show up, he was always late. More important, Rivera disagreed with the party's policy. At that time, Mexico was in turmoil, and the leaders of the Communist Party, representing the workers and farmers, planned to overthrow the government. Rivera was friendly with government officials and accepted commissions from them. The Communists thought he was a traitor. But even though he was no longer a member of the party, Rivera continued to sympathize with the working class and to think of himself as one of them.

The artist's fame had been growing in the United States for some time. Ameri-

Rivera, happily at work on a mural, poses for a photograph with an unidentified dog.

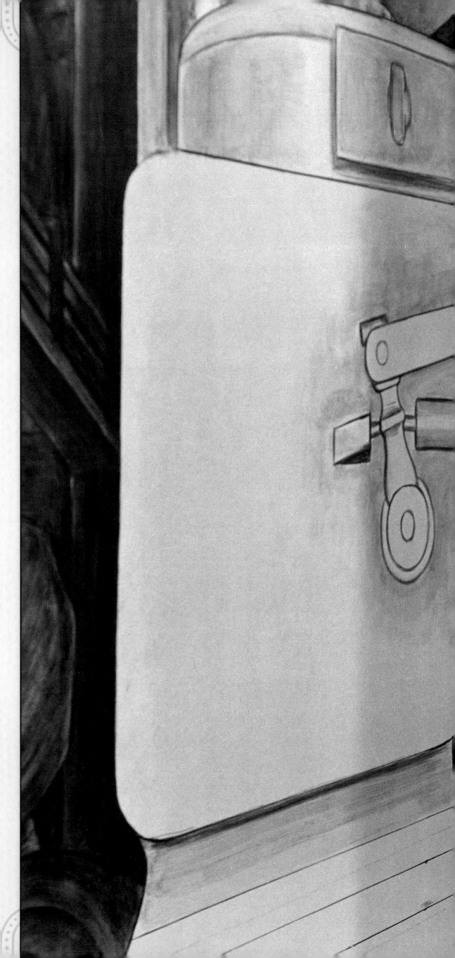

can collectors returned from Mexico with his paintings of flower carriers burdened with huge baskets of blossoms and Indian girls in *trenzas*, or braids, selling armfuls of calla lilies. An old friend from Rivera's Paris days, the sculptor Ralph Stackpole, brought two of Rivera's paintings home to San Francisco. Stackpole gave one to William Gerstle, president of the San Francisco Art Commission. Gerstle didn't like the picture but hung it in his studio anyway. "To my surprise I couldn't take my eyes off it," he said, and he donated money for Rivera to paint a mural in the California School of Fine Arts (later renamed the San Francisco Art Institute).

When Rivera received the offer, he said, "I was enormously excited. This would be a crucial test of my mural techniques. Unlike Mexico, the United States was a truly industrial country . . . [and] the ideal place for modern mural art."

On November 10, 1930, Rivera and Frida arrived in San Francisco. They were warmly welcomed and invited to parties, receptions, and even a football game, where they attracted more attention than the players on the field. Huge Rivera sat there in his Stetson hat making endless sketches, while tiny Frida charmed everyone by wearing clothes typical of a Tehuana Indian—a colorful long skirt, serape, dangling earrings, chunky bead necklace, and sandals. During her stay in San Francisco, Frida painted many portraits of friends and patrons and completed a wedding portrait of herself and Rivera that was to become one of her best-known works. Rivera gave lectures in French and Spanish, and thousands gathered to hear him. He carried a notebook and sketched people he met; they later became part of his mural.

Rivera's School of Fine Arts project, *The Making of a Fresco Showing the Building of a City*, is a mural within a mural. The panels, like illustrations in a picture book, reveal Rivera's process, step by step. "It was here that I showed how a mural is actually painted,"

The Flower Carrier, 1935. Rivera devoted many paintings of common people going about their day-to-day lives, like this worker straining with a load of flowers for the market.

The Making of a Fresco Showing the Building of a City, 1931. Rivera included his assistants sitting and kneeling on the scaffolding above and below him, illustrating how they worked together.

he said. Again using the artistic technique of trompe l'oeil, Rivera made the scaffolding look like real wood. But it is painted on the plaster as part of the fresco. When he was in Italy, Rivera had learned about the period called the Renaissance, which lasted from approximately 1350 to 1550. Artists of that time had painted portraits of their patrons—the people who paid for the art—in the actual frescoes. Following the Renaissance tradition, Rivera portrayed his patrons in the central panel on the bottom. William Gerstle stands in the middle, examining plans for the fresco. Rivera even included himself sitting on the scaffolding in the upper center, holding a paintbrush and palette, his back to the viewer. "Since I was facing and leaning toward my work," he said, "the portrait of myself was a rear view with my buttocks protruding over the edge of the scaffold." Some people later criticized Rivera's "fat rear (very realistically painted)." But Rivera was merely poking fun at himself.

A glimpse of the mural within the mural shows a gigantic figure of a worker. On a side panel, smaller figures are building a skyscraper. Rivera wanted to illustrate how a modern city should be constructed. When he finished the mural, he signed it with the date, "Mayo 31, 1931," and he and Frida left for Mexico.

That summer he joyfully accepted an invitation to have a one-man retrospective, a show devoted exclusively to his work, at the new Museum of Modern Art (MoMA) in New York City. "To every modern artist," said Rivera, "this is the pinnacle of professional success."

Rivera had also accepted a commission from the Detroit Institute of Arts (DIA) to decorate the walls in their Garden Court. He had met William Valentiner, the director of DIA, in San Francisco. Valentiner thought that Rivera's storytelling style of painting and his interest in machinery would make him the perfect muralist to portray Detroit. The city was home to the American automobile industry and a manufacturing center with thousands of factories.

So in November, Rivera and Frida sailed to New York, their first stop. His show at MoMA opened in December 1931 and was a huge success. During the first two weeks, more than thirty thousand visitors flocked to see his paintings. After the show ended, Rivera and Frida took the train to Detroit.

At that time, America was in the midst of the Great Depression, and many people were out of work, hungry, and homeless. This was true in Detroit as well, but Rivera did not want to portray these grim realities. Instead, he planned to celebrate Detroit's industries.

The artist met with his patron, Edsel Ford, the president of the Ford Motor Company. Edsel's father, Henry, had established a giant automotive plant at the River Rouge where cars were mass-produced on an assembly line. Edsel Ford loved art as well as cars and excitedly discussed the mural.

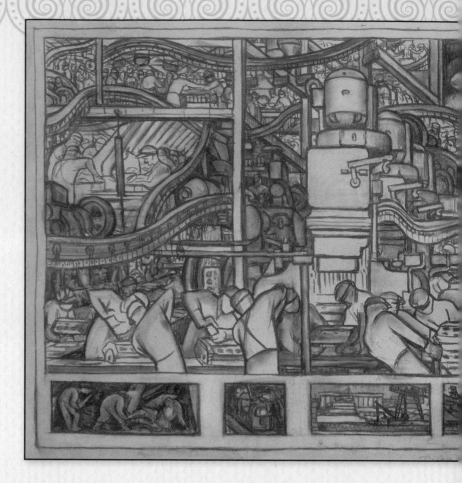

Rivera spent a month studying and sketching at the Rouge and at the Chrysler Motor Company and the Parke-Davis chemical plant. Frida often went with him. In the huge workshops, Rivera closely observed conveyor belts and precision instruments and asked questions about them. Edsel gave him a 1932 Ford sedan so he could travel around Detroit. Since Rivera didn't know how to drive, one of his assistants drove him. Frida, however, took driving lessons.

"I was afire with enthusiasm," said Rivera. "My childhood passion for mechanical toys had been transmuted to a delight in machinery for its own sake and for its meaning to man."

By May 1932, Rivera had presented his preliminary pencil drawings for the north and south walls to Edsel and Valentiner. Ford was astonished at the accuracy of Rivera's depiction of machinery in motion and at his understanding of the workers' jobs. Although Rivera had been hired to paint two walls in the Garden Court, he now proposed filling all four walls to carry out his design. Ford agreed and increased Rivera's payment.

The *Detroit Industry* murals: *Presentation Drawing of North Wall Automotive Panel*, 1932. The charcoal drawing depicts the workers producing the engine and transmission of a 1932 Ford V-8 automobile.

Rivera enlarged his compositions and drew "cartoons" in charcoal that were the actual size of the panels. Then the outlines were transferred to the walls, and Rivera painted them in black. In July, he began painting in full color. At night, his assistants applied two coats of plaster to make the walls ready for Rivera in the morning. Sometimes he arrived later than expected, which made the plasterers worry that the plaster would dry out. Rivera liked to dawdle by reading the comics in the newspaper or talking to friends. He said he wanted to wait till the last minute before painting in order to keep his work fresh and spontaneous. Once he began, he painted for twelve to fourteen hours straight. Frida often brought lunch to him in a big Mexican basket. She had found a few Mexican grocery stores that sold his favorite foods.

Rivera wanted her to stay in the hotel and paint. She was pregnant, and doctors advised her to rest because of her delicate health. Rivera even arranged for a young

artist, Lucienne Bloch, to move into their suite and encourage Frida to paint. In July, she had a miscarriage and was rushed to the hospital. She expressed her grief over the loss of the baby in drawings and paintings that Rivera termed "a series of masterpieces."

In September, Frida received word that her mother was dying, and she left for Mexico City. When she returned in October, Rivera met her at the train station. At first Frida didn't recognize him because he had lost so much weight while she was gone. He had missed her, her painting, and her cooking.

Rivera continued work on the mural, proceeding from section to section. A panel on the north wall shows figures in insectlike gas masks working with chemicals. They are making a poisonous gas bomb, which is pictured behind them. Gas bombs had been used in the Great War, and Rivera wanted to show the destructive side of chemistry as well as the good.

Below this, in the largest panel, Rivera

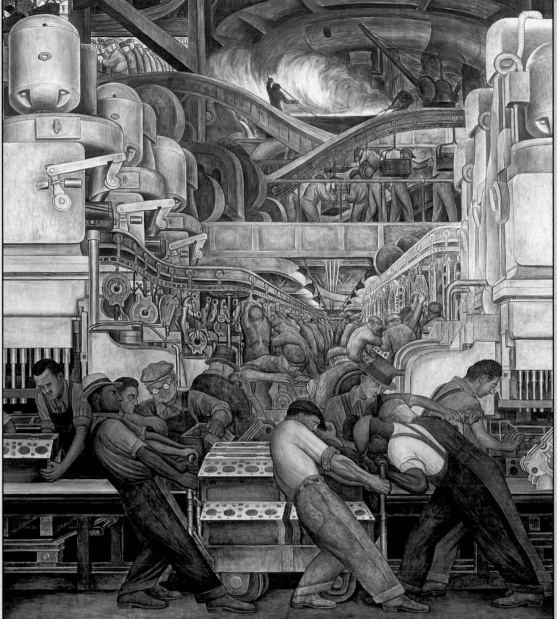

OPPOSITE:
Manufacture of Poisonous Gas Bombs, 1932. A "cartoon" drawn in charcoal is the actual size of the panel in the fresco (top). The outlines were transferred to the wall. Rivera then painted the figures and used pigments from the United States, Mexico, and France to obtain lasting colors (bottom).

LEFT: *Production and Manufacture of Engine and Transmission, Detroit Industry,* 1933. In this detail of the north wall, Rivera portrayed men of all races and ages working hard together.

portrayed multiracial workers producing the engine and transmission of a Ford V-8 automobile. Again conforming to Renaissance tradition, he included a small self-portrait of himself, wearing a bowler hat, standing among a group of workers in the background. On the south wall, he painted portraits of his sponsors, Ford and Valentiner. Valentiner holds the dedication paper, which begins, "These frescoes, painted between July 25, 1932, and March 13, 1933 . . . are the gift to the city of Detroit."

A few days before the public unveiling of the frescoes, there was a private showing for Detroit art patrons and critics. The result was a series of attacks that appeared in the newspapers. An editorial in the *Detroit News* criticized the frescoes as "foolishly vulgar" and "un-American."

Society ladies were shocked to see factories depicted in their "lovely garden." They asked Rivera why he "had not chosen something pleasanter to paint instead." But factory workers were delighted and thanked Rivera. A group of engineers declared that every inch of his work was "technically correct."

On Sunday, March 26, 1933, the frescoes were opened to the public, and ten thousand people jammed the court. Valentiner spoke to the crowds and defended the frescoes. "Edsel Ford, the donor, was completely satisfied," he said.

A photograph of the entire *Detroit Industry* north wall, which includes *The Red and Black Races, Manufacture of Poisonous Gas Bombs,* and *Production and Manufacture of Engine and Transmission*, 1933, shows how Rivera used architectural elements of the courtyard to frame the panels of the fresco.

Ford himself said, "I admire Rivera's spirit. I really believe he was trying to express the spirit of Detroit."

Rivera later said, "I was gratified that Edsel Ford stood by me loyally . . . The overwhelming approval of my paintings by the workers of Detroit . . . seemed to be the beginning of the realization of my life's dream."

While he was still in Detroit, Rivera had begun making sketches for his next project. He had been commissioned to paint a mural in the lobby of the new Radio Corporation of America (RCA) office building under construction at Rockefeller Center in New York City. "The theme offered me was an exciting one," said Rivera. "'Man at the Crossroads Looking with Hope and High Vision to the Choosing of a New and Better Future.'"

He wrote an outline describing his intended paintings. The center of his mural would feature a worker at the controls of a large machine. He submitted the outline with his sketches. Raymond Hood, the architect of the building, sent Rivera a telegram that read, "Sketch approved by Mr. Rockefeller . . . Can go right ahead with larger scale."

In March 1933, Rivera and Frida went to New York. Frida had become close friends with Abby Aldrich Rockefeller, a collector of modern art who had urged her son Nelson to hire Rivera as a muralist for the RCA Building. "I set to work immediately," said Rivera. "I painted rapidly and easily. Everything was going smoothly—perhaps too smoothly." Although Rockefeller had not yet viewed Rivera's fresco in person, he saw a picture of it in the Sunday newspaper and liked it.

The building was due to open on May 1, and Rivera worked at breakneck speed to complete the mural. By the end of April he was almost done. But he had changed one of the figures into a portrait of Vladimir Lenin, the leader of the Communist Party of the Soviet Union. Lenin's portrait had not been included in the original sketch.

Nelson Rockefeller came to see Rivera's mural and on May 4 sent him a note. The portrait of Lenin was "beautifully painted," wrote Rockefeller, but it might "offend a great many people." So he asked Rivera to paint out Lenin's face and "substitute the face of some unknown man."

Rivera refused.

On May 9, Rivera was paid his entire fee and fired. The mural was covered with canvas. "Hostilities broke out," said Rivera. American artists expressed outrage on his behalf. People picketed the building and demanded that the mural be uncovered, while policemen on horseback patrolled the streets. Rivera gave a speech at a rally and spoke on the radio. He hired a photographer to make a record of his mural, but guards barred the way. Lucienne Bloch, now one of Rivera's assistants, sneaked a small Leica camera into her blouse and snapped as many photos as she could.

Angry that he had been fired, Rivera used some of the money to do another mural in New York City. He selected a shabby old building on West Fourteenth Street that was the home of the New Workers' School. At first he thought he would duplicate the Rockefeller Center mural, but it was not suitable for the space. So he began a new work on movable panels titled *Portrait of America*. In December, when it was finished, he and Frida sailed to Mexico.

Meanwhile, Nelson Rockefeller planned to transfer the mural from the RCA Building to the Museum of Modern Art. But at midnight on Saturday, February 9, 1934, workers with axes smashed the mural to bits. It was believed that Rockefeller had given the order. However, the artist Ben Shahn, who assisted Rivera and who had been there when Rivera was fired, claimed that the building's architect, Raymond Hood, and his associates were responsible.

Rivera was devastated when he heard the news. Depressed and exhausted, he became ill for a long period of time. He feared that an "eye ailment" might blind him. "Poor health kept me from painting murals for several years," he wrote.

The Flower Vendor (*Girl with Lilies*), 1941. Rivera painted many versions of girls and women holding and selling calla lilies, one of his favorite themes.

Gradually, however, he started sketching and painting again, and he produced *The Flower Carrier* and versions of pigtailed women holding huge bunches of calla lilies.

Rivera still loved the ladies, and the ladies still loved him. Frida overlooked most of his affairs, but when he became involved with her sister, Cristina, she left him. Frida moved out of the twin houses and studios they had built in San Angel, a section of Mexico City.

"I never was . . . a faithful husband," admitted Rivera. "And yet I knew I could not change."

He and Frida divorced. But they never stopped caring about each other.

In 1940, Rivera accepted a commission to paint a mural for an exposition on Treasure Island in San Francisco. By this time, World War II had erupted in Europe. Rivera predicted that the United States would become involved. If that happened, he hoped that his mural would promote cooperation among North and South American countries in fighting against the Axis powers.

While he worked on his mural, Frida arrived in San Francisco. She was sick and in pain, suffering from past injuries. Rivera felt deeply concerned. He begged her to remarry him. Finally she agreed but insisted on certain conditions. "I was so happy to have Frida back," said Rivera, "that I assented to everything, and on my fifty-fourth birthday, December 8, 1940, Frida and I were married for the second time."

When they returned to Mexico, Rivera resumed work on the mural in the National Palace. His true love, always, was painting for and about his people.

At this time, he also started building Anahuacalli, a place to showcase his collection of pre-Columbian art. By now, he had more than sixty thousand objects. He chose a site on a lava bed near Coyoacán, and Frida helped him cut stone for the square-shaped building, designed in an Aztec-Mayan style. During World War II Rivera and Frida lived there. After the war, Anahuacalli became a museum that Rivera gave to the Mexican people.

For a long time, Rivera received no offers to paint murals. Originally intended to teach the illiterate masses about their culture, murals had been replaced by movies with sound. Now people crowded the movie theaters on Saturdays rather than look at art.

Then during the late 1940s, American and European tourists thronged Mexico. Europe was still rebuilding after the war, and instead of vacationing there, visitors came to Mexico. The hotel business boomed. Rivera was commissioned to create a mural in the dining room of the new Hotel del Prado in Mexico City. The hotel faced Alameda Park. He said, "The theme I chose was 'A Sunday in Alameda Park.' In the painting, I attempted to combine my own childhood experiences in the park with scenes and personages associated with its history." The mural covered the dining room's entire wall, which was about fifty feet long and sixteen feet high.

In the center, Rivera portrayed himself as a chubby ten-year-old in knickers.

Dream of A Sunday Afternoon in Alameda Park, 1947–48. A detail of the mural shows Rivera as a boy in striped socks and a straw hat holding the hand of *La Catrina,* in a plumed hat. Posada, in a suit and bowler hat, walks on the other side of her. Frida Kahlo, pictured as a grown-up, stands behind Rivera with one hand on his shoulder.

39

He holds the hand of "Death," a skeleton wearing a woman's dress and a boa made of withered ears of corn. She looks exactly like the caricature *La Catrina* created by Rivera's admired teacher, José Guadalupe Posada. Art critics declared that the mural, titled *Dream of a Sunday Afternoon in Alameda Park,* was Rivera's masterpiece.

In 1949, the National Institute of Fine Arts in Mexico City organized a retrospective of his work in the Palace of Fine Arts. Collectors from all over the world—even Nelson Rockefeller—loaned their Rivera paintings for the exhibition.

In 1951, a catalog was published in conjunction with the retrospective. Frida wrote an essay in tribute to her husband. "To Diego painting is everything," she wrote. "He prefers his work to anything else in the world . . . He especially loves the Indians . . . for their elegance, their beauty, and because they are the living flower of the cultural tradition of America . . . This love he has conveyed in painting after painting."

Rivera was diagnosed with cancer in 1952. He changed his diet and underwent X-ray treatments. He was temporarily cured, but the cancer returned a couple of years later. Rivera traveled to Moscow, Russia, for experimental treatment. "As I lay in the hospital," he said, "I tried to sum up the memory of my life . . . All I could say was that the most joyous moments of my life were those I had spent in painting."

In September 1957, Rivera suffered a stroke and lost the use of his right arm. He still attempted to paint but said, "The brush no longer obeys me."

The "genial cannibal," Diego Rivera, died of heart failure in his studio in San Angel on November 24, 1957, at the age of seventy. Near his bed stood two easels holding unfinished paintings. When he returned from Russia several years earlier, he had dictated the last words of his autobiography. "Now I am home again," he had said. "Right now my fingers and I are literally itching to start work on my next mural." •

Rivera painting at an easel in his studio.

A NOTE ABOUT THE HISTORY OF MEXICO, AS REFERENCED IN RIVERA'S ARTWORK

Many of Rivera's themes and concepts are based on or influenced by historical and contemporary events in Mexico. What is now Mexico was the center of flourishing Indian cultures before the arrival of Columbus in the New World. In 1521, the Spanish under Hernán Cortés conquered the Aztec capital of Tenochtitlan, which at the time was the largest city in the world. The Aztecs had a highly developed civilization and complex religious beliefs. Yet the Catholic Church converted most of the Indians to Christianity. The Indian population made up the lowest rung of society and worked as slaves for the Spanish landowners. Many Indians died from diseases, such as smallpox, that the Europeans brought with them. The Spaniards ruled Mexico until the Mexican War of Independence ended in 1821.

For almost a century, Mexico was wracked by continual fighting. From 1846 to 1848, Mexico fought a war with the United States, which resulted in a loss of half the country. Much of the western United States, including California, Nevada, Utah, and Texas, once belonged to Mexico.

In the 1860s, France invaded Mexico and attempted to gain control. However, on May 5, 1862, the Mexican army defeated the French army at the city of Puebla. The battle is still considered the foremost symbol of Mexican patriotism and is celebrated as Cinco de Mayo, or "the fifth of May."

In 1877, Porfirio Díaz overthrew the government and became president. Díaz was a cruel dictator who favored large landowners and foreign commercial interests. He was in power for thirty-four years. Diego Rivera was born in 1886. Like many other young educated or artistic Mexicans of his time, he grew up to be a strong nationalist. He opposed the influence of foreign countries in Mexico as well as injustices toward the peasants and workers. Rivera later claimed that he took part in the revolt against Díaz, but on November 20, 1910, the day Francisco I. Madero challenged Díaz and proclaimed the beginning of the Mexican Revolution, Rivera was exhibiting his artwork at San Carlos Academy. The long and bloody Mexican Revolution lasted for seven years. One leader after another took control. During the revolution, Rivera lived and painted in Paris and traveled to Italy to study frescoes.

A constitution was finally signed in Mexico on January 31, 1917. Álvaro Obregón, the greatest general of the revolution, was elected president in 1920. Obregón's education minister, José Vasconcelos, took a keen interest in the arts as a way of promoting Mexican culture. He organized the mural program and invited Rivera to participate upon his return to Mexico in 1921.

After four years in office, President Obregón was replaced by Plutarco Calles. Obregón later planned to run for reelection, but on July 17, 1928, he was assassinated. Calles assumed power behind the scenes and arranged for Emilio Portes Gil to become interim president. During this time, Rivera had left for a visit to the Soviet Union.

When Rivera returned in May 1928, Mexico was in a state of turmoil. The gap between the rich and the poor had widened. Left-wing unionists clashed with right-wing fascists. Vasconcelos, the educator who had sponsored the mural program, had run for president in 1924, but Calles had defeated him. Starting in 1929, the world wide economic depression gripped Mexico. Banks collapsed. People lost their jobs and went hungry while the rich grew richer. By now, most Mexicans accepted a one-party democracy, and the Partido Revolucionario Institucional (PRI) was formed.

In 1934, a new president, Lázaro Cárdenas, was elected. Cárdenas sent Calles into exile and sided with the poor and the oppressed. He distributed land to the *campesinos*, the peasants. Gradually, the Indian population gained greater access to education and health services. In 1938, President Cárdenas nationalized the Mexican oil industry. The economy improved, and Mexico became modernized. Cárdenas was regarded as the best president of Mexico since the revolution.

In 1940, Ávila Camacho took office, and Mexico joined the war against Japan and Germany. During World War II, Mexican pilots trained in the United States. Following the end of the war in 1945, the Mexican government focused on economic growth.

When Miguel Alemán Valdés became president in 1946, he encouraged tourism as a business. During this period, Rivera created his mural *Dream of a Sunday Afternoon in Alameda Park* in the new Hotel del Prado in Mexico City. President Valdés urged him to sell easel paintings to visiting tourists.

In 1952, Adolfo Ruiz Cortines was elected president. One of his most important achievements was to grant voting rights to women. During his presidency, Cortines approved the plan to honor Rivera with a retrospective. Cortines was president when Rivera died on November 24, 1957. Rivera's body was taken to the Rotunda of the Palace of Fine Arts. Then, according to Rivera's wishes, he was cremated. President Cortines ordered that Rivera's ashes be placed in the Rotonda de los Hombres Ilustres (Rotunda of Illustrious Men) in Mexico City, where the urn now rests.

A NOTE ABOUT RIVERA'S ARTISTIC INFLUENCES

It is not possible for every artwork mentioned to be reproduced within these pages, nor to include examples from every artist and culture referenced. Therefore, I encourage you to view these works via your library or the Internet.

Art is always changing, and what is popular at one time may not be at a later time, as new ways of thinking about art are introduced. Sometimes these new ways are widely accepted, and sometimes they take a while to become popular. Diego Rivera's art training at San Carlos Academy from 1898 to 1906 emphasized what was considered popular and standard for that time *in Europe* and excluded discussion of art created in the Americas. Rivera was instructed in drawing from life and photographs, learning perspective and laws of proportion, and painting figures and landscapes in a realistic style.

In Madrid, Spain, Rivera went to the Prado Museum and studied works by the Old Masters, who also painted in a primarily realistic style: El Greco (1541–1614), Velázquez (1599–1660), and Goya (1746–1828). In Paris he admired modern paintings by Paul Cézanne (1839–1906). Although his early work was more realistic, Cézanne's later work was more abstract and inspired a new movement called Cubism, which began in the time Rivera was in Paris. The Cubists, led by Pablo Picasso, depicted subjects broken into angular pieces. The flat, geometric shapes were designed in an abstract pattern to show many views at once in a single painting. From 1913 to 1917, Rivera painted hundreds of pictures in the Cubist style.

When Rivera went to Italy in 1920, he studied frescoes that had been painted by Renaissance artists in the fifteenth and sixteenth centuries or even earlier. One of them was Giotto. In 1305, Giotto painted thirty-eight frescoes in watercolors directly onto the plaster walls of the Arena Chapel in Padua. Rivera visited the chapel and saw the frescoes in person. They influenced him more than any other Renaissance art. He adopted Giotto's style of "massing figures"—though he sometimes featured a solitary figure—and the use of common objects in order to give viewers a sense of something familiar. The frescoes Rivera saw in his travels in Italy were intended to instruct the common people, who could not read, about Christianity; in the same way, Rivera's frescoes in Mexico would teach his people the story of their country.

At home in Mexico, Rivera began collecting pre-Columbian art. These stone sculptures and ceramics had been created by the people native to Mexico—Olmecs, Toltecs, Mayas, and Aztecs—who lived there before Europeans arrived in the sixteenth century. Rivera revived respect for the Aztecs' highly developed civilization in his own country as well as outside. Although he incorporated techniques learned in the European tradition, like perspective and frescoes, Rivera's murals and easel paintings used pre-Columbian images to celebrate Mexico's history and Indian heritage—two very non-European traditions.

WHERE TO VIEW WORKS BY DIEGO RIVERA

Canada
Virtual Museum of Canada

England
Birmingham Museum and Art Gallery

Mexico
Hotel del Prado, Mexico City
Museo de Arte Moderno, Mexico City
Museo del Palacio de Bellas Artes, Mexico, D.F.
Museo Diego Rivera—Anahuacalli
Museo Diego Rivera, Guanajuato
Museo Frida Kahlo (The Blue House), Mexico City
Palacio de Cortés, Cuernavaca

United States
Art Institute of Chicago
City College of San Francisco
Detroit Institute of Arts
Los Angeles County Museum of Art
The Museum of Modern Art, New York
Norton Simon Museum, Pasadena, California
Pacific Stock Exchange Tower, San Francisco
Philadelphia Museum of Art
San Diego Museum of Art
San Francisco Art Institute
San Francisco Museum of Modern Art
Smith College Museum of Art, Northampton,
 Massachusetts

GLOSSARY

Aztec culture: The rites, religion, art, and architecture of the Native American people of Central Mexico, whose civilization was at its height at the time of the Spanish Conquest in the early sixteenth century.

caricatures: Pictures that exaggerate facial characteristics or details, sometimes as a form of ridicule.

cartoon: A full-scale design for a picture to be transferred to a fresco, canvas, or other surface.

Chicharro, Eduardo y Agüera (1873–1949): A fashionable Spanish painter of the early twentieth century who painted realistic portraits and still lifes in oils.

commission: An order for a work of art that is paid for.

Communist Party: A political party that supported the Soviet Union. In Mexico, the Communist Party advocated community-owned property and a government ruled by the working class.

composition: The arrangement or organization of shapes and lines on a two-dimensional surface, such as paper or canvas.

critics: People who evaluate and write about artistic works.

Cubism: A revolutionary school of art, started in 1907 by Pablo Picasso and Georges Braque, that broke the subject of a painting or sculpture into fragments and abstract patterns, sometimes even adding scraps of real materials in a technique that came to be known as collage.

draftsman: A person who is exceptionally skilled in drawing.

exhibition: A public display of the work of an artist or a group of artists.

folk artist: A person, usually self-taught or without any formal training, who creates art that reflects a particular culture or region.

frescoes: Artworks created by painting in watercolors directly onto fresh moist plaster.

Giotto (1267–1337): An early Renaissance Italian artist who painted lifelike figures in a departure from the flat style of the medieval period and is thus regarded as the founder of Western painting.

Goya, Francisco José de (1746–1828): A Spanish artist who painted religious and historical subjects and also portraits in a loose, personal style that led the way to modern European art.

Great Depression: A worldwide economic slump that started in 1929 with the American stock market collapse, which led to failed banks in the United States, Mexico, and other countries. Millions of people were left jobless, homeless, and hungry until the outbreak of World War II in 1939.

Greco, El (1541–1614): An artist, born in Crete, who studied in Italy and painted unique, elongated figures that expressed his intense religious feelings. Rivera studied and copied his work in the Prado Museum.

Hood, Raymond (1881–1934): A mid-twentieth-century American architect who designed a number of tall buildings in New York City, including the RCA Building, in a sleek, art deco style.

Kahlo, Frida (1907–54): A Mexican painter best known for her imaginative self-portraits filled with symbols and animals that told the dramatic story of her life and marriage to Rivera.

Louvre Museum: First built as a fortress, it became a museum open to the public in 1793. It is located in Paris and contains vast collections of sculptures, paintings, furniture, jewelry, and antiquities.

masterpiece: An artist's greatest work; a piece that demonstrates exceptional skill.

Mexican Muralism: A program, beginning in 1920, in which frescoes were painted on walls in public places by Mexican artists for the people of Mexico. The murals celebrated Mexican culture and history.

Michelangelo (1475–1564): A late Renaissance Italian painter and sculptor who created masterpieces that idealized human forms, such as the fresco on the ceiling of the Sistine Chapel in Vatican City (Rome).

mural: A large picture painted directly on a wall.

Orozco, José Clemente (1883–1949): A Mexican painter who promoted the political causes of peasants and workers in his art. With Rivera, he was a leader of the movement known as Mexican Muralism.

palette: Usually a flat piece of wood with a thumbhole, used to hold the different colors needed for a painting.

panels: Flat pieces of wood or sections of a wall on which pictures are painted.

patron: A person who supports an artist with money or gifts.

Picasso, Pablo (1881–1973): A Spanish-born artist considered a giant of the twentieth century because of his enormous productivity; the many styles he developed, from his own Blue Period and Rose Period to Cubism and Expressionism; and his mastery of a wide variety of media.

pigments: Ground powders made from plants or minerals that are mixed with water or saliva and a binder such as chalk or egg to form a paste that gives color to paint.

portrait: A painting or drawing of a person or animal that captures a physical likeness or reveals character and inner spirit.

Pre-Columbian sculptures: Figures of people, animals, and deities created in stone and clay by the ancient Olmecs, Toltecs, Aztecs, and Mayas who were native to Mexico.

retrospective: An art exhibit that showcases an entire period or an entire lifetime of an artist's work.

scaffold: A temporary platform used by artists when working on a tall structure.

sculpture: A three-dimensional artwork that has depth as well as width and height and occupies real space.

Shahn, Ben (1898–1969): A Lithuanian-born American artist who was trained in lithography and who often combined text and images to express his concerns about workers' rights, injustice, immigration, and modern urban life.

Siqueiros, David Alfaro (1896–1974): A Mexican social realist painter known for his murals who met Rivera in Paris and traveled to Italy with him to study the frescoes of the Renaissance.

Soviet Union: A group of fifteen republics, including Russia (the largest), the Ukraine, and Belorussia (now Belarus), that was formed in 1922 under Vladimir Lenin and the Communist Party following the Russian Civil War (ca. 1917–21).

Stackpole, Ralph (1885–1973): An American sculptor, painter, muralist, and art educator who became friends with Rivera in Paris and helped bring him to the United States.

studio: The workroom of an artist.

trompe l'oeil: A technique to fool the eye into thinking that a flat surface is three-dimensional; a tradition in art history.

Uccello, Paolo (1397–1475): An Italian artist of the early Renaissance who used the new science of perspective to create the illusion of depth on a flat, two-dimensional surface.

Velázquez, Diego (1599–1660): A seventeenth-century Spanish artist known for his realistic portraits, still lifes, and religious subjects, which were painted with vigorous brushstrokes and a varied palette. Rivera studied and copied his work.

SOURCE NOTES

page 5: "I was . . . three hundred pounds." Diego Rivera, *My Art, My Life: An Autobiography,* with Gladys March (New York: Dover Publications, 1991), 25.

page 5: "People I love . . . like a frog." Rivera, 181.

page 5: "the genial cannibal." Marevna Vorobiev, quoted in Patrick Marnham, *Dreaming with His Eyes Open: A Life of Diego Rivera* (Berkeley: University of California Press, 1998), 95.

page 5: "restless, dissatisfied, impatient." Rivera, 41.

page 5: "academic and empty." Rivera, 31.

page 5: "What I knew . . . Mexico." Rivera, 67.

page 5: "The new art . . . public buildings." Rivera, 66.

page 5: "And so . . . mural painting." Rivera, 66.

page 5: "The secret . . . is Mexican." Rivera, 31.

page 6: "As far back . . . furniture." Rivera, 9.

page 6: "studio." Rivera, 9.

page 6: "Here I made . . . 'murals.'" Rivera, 9.

page 7: "the engineer. " Rivera, 9.

page 7: "They would take me . . . the whistle." Rivera, 9.

page 7: "We sent her . . . little box." Station agent, quoted in Bertram D. Wolfe, *The Fabulous Life of Diego Rivera* (New York: First Cooper Square Press, 2000), 21.

page 7: "I began . . . to read." Rivera, 4.

page 7: "The home we found . . . neighborhood." Rivera, 10.

page 8: "The further I progressed . . . old Mexican art." Rivera, 16.

page 10: "It was he . . . Mexican people." Rivera, 18.

page 10: "We Veracruzanos . . . appreciate art." Don Teodoro A. Dehesa, quoted in Wolfe, 41.

page 10: "ordinary-size Spanish hat." Rivera, 29.

page 12: "Suddenly, I . . . my people." Rivera, 39.

page 12: "revolutionary." Rivera, 58.

page 13: "There was no money . . . or medicine." Rivera, 70.

page 13: "This innocent death . . . depressed me." Rivera, 70.

page 13: "Life was changing . . . the same." Rivera, 66.

page 13: "new career . . . mural painter." Rivera, 71.

page 13: "I went to Italy . . . old masters." Rivera, 71.

page 14: "The call . . . than ever." Rivera, 72.

page 14: "All the colors . . . luminous child." Rivera, 72.

page 14: "The very first . . . and contentedly." Rivera, 72.

page 14: "At last . . . University of Mexico." Rivera, 73.

page 16: "free art schools . . . remarkable productions." Rivera, 78.

page 16: "Here, the people . . . lively fiestas." Rivera, 80.

page 16: "As my work . . . wall surfaces." Rivera, 80.

page 17: "If, as sometimes . . . the next day." Rivera, 81.

page 18: "I, unfortunately . . . to resist." Rivera, 83.

page 19: "Diego, please . . . from there!" Frida Kahlo, quoted in Rivera, 102.

page 19: "thick eyebrows . . . of a blackbird." Rivera, 102.

page 21: "I want . . . opinion." Frida Kahlo, quoted in Rivera, 102.

page 21: "The canvases . . . of expression." Rivera, 102.

page 21: "It was obvious . . . authentic artist." Rivera, 103.

page 21: "You have a dog-face." Rivera, quoted in Wolfe, 244.

page 21: "And you . . . a frog!" Frida Kahlo, quoted in Wolfe, 244.

page 21: "I might leave . . . and changes." Rivera, 101.

page 25: "To my surprise . . . off it." William Gerstle, quoted in Wolfe, 280–81.

page 25: "I was enormously . . . modern mural art." Rivera, 105.

page 25: "It was here . . . actually painted." Rivera, 108.

page 27: "Since I was . . . the scaffold." Rivera, 108.

page 27: "fat rear (very realistically painted)." Kenneth Callahan, quoted in Wolfe, 292.

page 27: "Mayo 31, 1931." Marnham, 236.

page 27: "To every modern artist . . . professional success." Rivera, 109.

page 28: "I was afire . . . meaning to man." Rivera, 111–12.

page 30: "a series of masterpieces." Rivera, 123.

page 31: "These frescoes . . . city of Detroit." Linda Bank Downs, *Diego Rivera: The Detroit Industry Murals* (New York: W. W. Norton & Company, 1999), 35.

page 32: "foolishly vulgar . . . un-American." *Detroit News,* quoted in Downs, 174.

page 32: "lovely garden." Rivera, 119.

page 32: "had not chosen . . . to paint instead." Rivera, 119.

page 32: "technically correct." Rivera, 120.

page 32: "Edsel Ford . . . completely satisfied." William Valentiner, quoted in Downs, 177.

page 34: "I admire Rivera's . . . spirit of Detroit." Edsel Ford, quoted in Wolfe, 314.

page 34: "I was gratified . . . my life's dream." Rivera, 122.

page 34: "The theme . . . Better Future.'" Rivera, 125.

page 34: "Sketch approved . . . larger scale." Raymond Hood, quoted in Wolfe, 323.

page 34: "I set to work . . . too smoothly." Rivera, 125.

page 35: "beautifully painted . . . some unknown man." Nelson A. Rockefeller, quoted in Wolfe, 325.

page 35: "Hostilities broke out." Rivera, quoted in Wolfe, 327.

page 35: "eye ailment." Rivera, 131.

page 35: "Poor health . . . several years." Rivera, 136.

page 37: "I never was . . . could not change." Rivera, 138.

page 37: "I was so happy . . . the second time." Rivera, 150.

page 38: "The theme I chose . . . its history." Rivera, 157.

page 40: "To Diego painting . . . painting after painting." Statement by Frida Kahlo, quoted in Rivera, 188.

page 40: "As I lay . . . spent in painting." Rivera, 180.

page 40: "The brush no longer obeys me." Rivera, quoted in Wolfe, 412.

page 40: "Now I am . . . my next mural." Rivera, 181.

page 44: "Massing of figures." Pete Hamill, *Diego Rivera* (New York: Abrams Books, 1999), 76.

51

BIBLIOGRAPHY

*Denotes material suitable for younger readers.

Downs, Linda Bank. *Diego Rivera: The Detroit Industry Murals*. New York: W. W. Norton & Company, 1999.

Hamill, Pete. *Diego Rivera*. New York: Abrams, 1999.

Helms, Cynthia Newman, ed. *Diego Rivera: A Retrospective*. New York: Founders Society, Detroit Institute of Arts, in association with W. W. Norton & Company, 1986.

*Holzhery, Magdelena. *Frida Kahlo: The Artist in the Blue House*, trans. Ishbel Flett. Munich: Prestel Verlag, 2003.

Kettenmann, Andrea. *Rivera*. London: Taschen, 2006.

*Marín, Guadalupe Rivera, and Diego Rivera. *My Papa Diego and Me*. San Francisco: Children's Book Press, 2009.

Marnham, Patrick. *Dreaming with His Eyes Open: A Life of Diego Rivera*. Berkeley: University of California Press, 1998.

Rivera, Diego. *My Art, My Life: An Autobiography*. With Gladys March. New York: Dover Publications, Inc., 1991.

Shorris, Earl. *The Life and Times of Mexico*. New York: W. W. Norton & Company, 2004.

Wolfe, Bertram D. *The Fabulous Life of Diego Rivera*. New York: First Cooper Square Press, 2000.

ACKNOWLEDGMENTS

I am deeply grateful to my editor, Howard Reeves, for believing in the importance of this book and pursuing publication. At Abrams I also thank Jenna Pocius and Brett Wright for their dedicated work at the start, Maria Middleton for her great skill in designing this book, Melissa Faulner in editorial, Jennifer Graham in managing editorial, Alison Gervais in production, and Jason Wells and Laura Mihalick in marketing.

My heartfelt thanks to Blenda and Joe Polito for their hospitality and assistance during the days I was researching at the Detroit Institute of Arts.

I especially want to express my gratitude to Tony and Roger Johnston and to Dana Goldberg, executive editor at Children's Book Press, for helping me proceed with permissions to reproduce the art of Diego Rivera.

My sincerest thanks to Jim Nikas for contributing prints by José Posada for this book.

Most of all, I thank George Nicholson for encouraging me to bring the art of Diego Rivera to children. And a big thank-you to his assistant, Erica Rand Silverman. A bouquet of thanks to my friends, the writers of Lunch Bunch, for their helpful critiques. And last but certainly not least, I thank my husband, Michael, for viewing Rivera's art with me and sharing my enjoyment.

ART CREDITS

Page 4: *Self-Portrait*, 1941. Oil on canvas, 24 x 16 ⅞ in. Smith College Museum of Art, Northampton, MA. **Page 6:** Diego Rivera at the age of four with his toy train, ca. 1890. **Page 7:** *The Boy with the Taco* (*El niño del taco*), 1932. Print, lithograph, 17 x 11 ⅞ in. Courtesy of the Los Angeles County Museum of Art, Los Angeles, CA. **Page 9:** Top: *La Calavera Catrina* by José Guadalupe Posada, 1913. Zinc etching, 5 x 6 in. Bottom: *El jarabe en ultratumba* by José Guadalupe Posada, ca. 1910. Zinc etching, 5 ½ x 8 in. **Page 11:** *Las Meninas*, by Diego Rodriguez de Silva y Velázquez, ca. 1656. Oil on canvas, 10 x 9 ft. Museo Nacional del Prado, Madrid, Spain. Bridgeman Art Library. **Page 15:** *Il sogno di Gioacchino* (*Joachim's Dream*), by Giotto di Bondone, ca. 1305. Fresco. Scrovegni (Arena) Chapel, Padua, Italy. **Page 17:** *Dance in Tehuantepec* (*Danza en Tehuantepec*), 1935. Drawing, charcoal and watercolor, 18 ¹⁵/₁₆ x 23 ⅞ in. Courtesy of the Los Angeles County Museum of Art, Los Angeles, CA. **Page 19:** *Epic of the Mexican People: History of Mexico from the Conquest to 1930* (detail: conquistadors attack the Aztecs). Fresco. Palacio Nacional, Mexico City, Mexico. **Page 20:** Diego Rivera and Frida Kahlo, by Peter A. Juley & Son, ca. 1930. Photograph, 8 x 10 in. Smithsonian American Art Museum, Washington, DC. Peter A. Juley & Son Collection. **Pages 22–23:** Diego Rivera with dog, by W. J. Settler, 1933. Photograph, silver print. Detroit Institute of Arts. Bridgeman Art Library. **Page 24:** *The Flower Carrier*, 1935. Oil and tempera on Masonite, 48 x 47 ¾ in. San Francisco Museum of Modern Art, Albert M. Bender Collection, gift of Albert M. Bender in memory of Caroline Walter. **Page 26:** *The Making of a Fresco Showing the Building of a City*, 1931. Fresco. Image © San Francisco Art Institute, gift of William Gerstle. **Pages 28–29:** *Presentation Drawing of the North Wall Automotive Panel* for the *Detroit Industry* mural, 1932. Charcoal on paper. Detroit Institute of Arts. Bridgeman Art Library. **Page 30:** Top: *Manufacture of Poisonous Gas Bombs*, cartoon for the north wall fresco, 1932. Charcoal on paper. Detroit Institute of Arts. Bridgeman Art Library. Bottom: *Manufacture of Poisonous Gas Bombs*, detail of the north wall fresco, 1932–33. Detroit Institute of Arts. Bridgeman Art Library. **Page 31:** *Production and Manufacture of Engine and Transmission, Detroit Industry* north wall detail, 1932–33. Fresco. Detroit Institute of Arts. Bridgeman Art Library. **Pages 32–33:** North wall of *Detroit Industry* mural, 1932–33. Fresco. Detroit Institute of Arts. Bridgeman Art Library. **Page 36:** *The Flower Vendor* (*Girl with Lilies*), 1941. Oil on Masonite, 48 x 48 in. Norton Simon Museum, Pasadena, CA. Gift of Mr. Cary Grant. **Pages 38–39:** *Dream of a Sunday Afternoon in Alameda Park* (detail), 1947–48. Oil on board. Originally in the Hotel del Prado, Mexico City, Mexico; now in the Museo Mural Diego Rivera, Mexico City due to the 1985 earthquake. **Page 41:** Untitled photograph of Rivera painting in his studio, by Hector Gorás. Photograph, gelatin silver print, 9 ½ x 7 ½ in. Courtesy of the Los Angeles Country Museum of Art, Los Angeles, CA.

INDEX

Italicized page numbers indicate illustrations and captions

Anahuacalli, 37
Aztecs, 18, *19*, 21, 42, 46

Barr, Alfred, 19
Beloff, Angelina, 12-14
Bloch, Lucienne, 30, 35

calaveras (lively skeletons), 8, *9*

California School of Fine Arts, 25–26
Calles, Plutarco, 43–44
Cárdenas, Lázaro, 44
Cézanne, Paul, 45–46
Chicharro, Eduardo, 10
Christianity, 8, *15*, 16, 42, 46
Communists, Communism, 16, 18–19, 22, 34
Cortines, Adolfo Ruiz, 44
Cubism, 12–13, 45–46

Day of the Dead (El Dia de los Muertos), 8, *9*
Dehesa, Teodoro A., 10–12
Detroit Institute of Arts (DIA), 27–34
Díaz, Porfirio, 12, 14, 43

54

Education Ministry, Mexican, 16, 18–19, 21
Europe, 13, 38, 42
    Rivera's art studies and, 5, 8–11, 45–46

Faure, Élie, 13
folk art, 8, *9*, 16, *17*
Ford, Edsel, 28, 31–34
Ford Motor Company, 28, *29*, 31
France, 10, 13, *31*, 42–43
frescoes, 13, *15*, 26, 43, 46

Gerstle, William, 25–26
Giotto, 14, 46
    Il sogno di Gioacchino (*Joachim's Dream*), *15*
Goya, Francisco José de, 10, 45
Great Depression, 27
Greco, El, 10, 45

Hood, Raymond, 34–35
Hotel del Prado, 38, 44

Indians, 12, 40
    in Mexican history, 42, 44
    in Rivera's art, 16, 25
Italy, 13–14, *15*, 26, 43, 46

Kahlo, Frida (second wife), 40
    Detroit trip of, 27–29
    husband's first meeting with, 19–21
    husband's marriage to, 21, 37
    husband's RCA Building mural and, 34–35
    illnesses and injuries of, 37
    paintings of, 21, 25, 30
    physical appearance of, 19, *20*, 21, 25, *39*
    pregnancy of, 29
    San Francisco trips of, 25–27, 37

Lenin, Vladimir, 34–35

Madrid, 10, *10*, 45
Mexican Revolution, 12, 14, 43–44
Mexican War of Independence, 42

Mexico, 35
    centenary of, 12
    history of, 12–14, 18–19, *19*, 21–22, 42–44
    lower classes of, 12, 14, 18, 22
    politics in, 12, 14–16, 21–22, 43–44
    Rivera's art studies and, 8–10, 12, 43, 45–46
    Rivera's mural painting in, 5, 13–16, *17*, 37–38
    tourism in, 38, 44
Mexico City, 30, 37–40
    Rivera's education in, 5, 7–8
    Rivera's mural painting and, 16, 18–19, *19*, 21–22,
        38–40, 43–44
Modotti, Tina, 18
mural paintings, mural painting, 5–6, 8, 13–19
    for California School of Fine Arts, 25–26
    Creation, 14–16
    Dance in Tehuantepec, 16, *17*
    Detroit Industry, 28–34, *28–33*
    Dream of a Sunday Afternoon in Alameda Park,
        38–40, *38–39*, 44
    Epic of the Mexican People, 19, *19*, 21–22
    frescoes and, 13, *15*, 26, 43, 46
    *The Making of a Fresco Showing the Building
        of a City*, 25–27, *26*
    Portrait of America, 35
    for RCA Building, 34–35
    and Rivera's art studies in Italy, 13–14, 43
    Rivera's techniques in, 16–18, 21, 26
Museum of Modern Art (MoMA), 19, 27, 35

National Institute of Fine Arts, 40
National Palace, 19, *19*, 21–22
National Preparatory School, 8, 14
New Workers' School, 35

Obregón, Álvaro, 14, 43
Orozco, José Clemente, 14–16

Palace of Fine Arts, 40, 44
Paris, 5, 10–12, 25, 45–46
Picasso, Pablo, 12, 46
Posada, José Guadalupe:

55

La Calavera Catrina, 8, 9
La Catrina, 8, *39*, 40
El jarabe en ultratumba (*The Folk Dance Beyond the Grave*), *9*
Rivera's relationship with, 8–10, 12, 14, 40
Prado Museum, 10, *10*, 45
pre-Columbian art, 18, 37, 46

Radio Corporation of America (RCA) Building, 34–35
Renaissance, *15*, 26, 46
Rich, Irene, *4*, 5
Rivera, Diego:
  ambitions of, 6–8
  art exhibited by, 12, 27, 40
  artistic influences on, 45–46
  birth of, 6
  childhood and adolescence of, 6–10, *6*, 28, 38–40, *38–39*
  children of, 13, 18
  criticisms of, 16, 22, 32
  death of, 40, 43
  divorces of, 18, 37
  education and art studies of, 5, 7–14, *10*, *15*, 25–26, 43, 45–46
  fame of, 22–25, 32, 40
  finances of, 10, 13, 18, 28, 35
  illnesses and injuries of, 6–7, 18, 35, 40
  love affairs of, 12–16, 18, 21, 37
  nicknames of, 7, 10, 21
  physical appearance of, *4*, 5, *6*, 10, 13, *20*, 21, 22–23, 25, *26*, 27, 30–31, 38–40, *38–39*, *41*
  politics of, 16, 18–19, 22, 34
  storytelling style of painting of, 27
Rivera, Diego, paintings and murals of:
  The Boy with the Taco, 6, 7
  Creation, 14–16
  Dance in Tehuantepec, 16, *17*
  Detroit Industry murals, 28–34, *28–33*
  The Distribution of Arms, 21
  Dream of a Sunday Afternoon in Alameda Park, 38–40, *38–39*, 44

Epic of the Mexican People, 19, *19*, 21–22
flower carrier paintings, 24–25, *25*, *36*, 37
The Making of a Fresco Showing the Building of a City, 25–27, *26*
Portrait of America, 35
Self Portrait, *4*, 5
Rivera, Lupe Marín (first wife), 14–16, 18
Rockefeller, Abby Aldrich, 34
Rockefeller, Nelson, 34–35, 40

San Carlos Academy of Fine Arts, 8–10, 12, 43, 45
San Francisco, Calif., 25–27, 37
Shahn, Ben, 35
Siqueiros, David, 14–16
Soviet Union, 18–19, 34, 40, 43
Spain, 10–12, 18, *19*, 21
Stackpole, Ralph, 25

trompe l'oeil (trick to fool the eye), 21, 26

Union of Technical Workers, Painters, and Sculptors, 16

Valdés, Miguel Alemán, 44
Valentiner, William, 27–28, 31
Vasconcelos, José, 14, 43
Velázquez, Diego, 10, 45
  Las meninas (*The Maids of Honor*), *10–11*

World War I, 13, 30
World War II, 37, 44

Zandunga, La, 16, *17*